The Power Of Poetry

Hopes & Dreams

Edited By Jenni Harrison

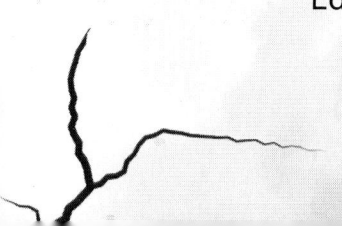

First published in Great Britain in 2023 by:

Young Writers
Remus House
Coltsfoot Drive
Peterborough
PE2 9BF
Telephone: 01733 890066
Website: www.youngwriters.co.uk

All Rights Reserved
Book Design by Ashley Janson
© Copyright Contributors 2022
Softback ISBN 978-1-80459-358-5

Printed and bound in the UK by BookPrintingUK
Website: www.bookprintinguk.com
YB0532E

FOREWORD

Since 1991, here at Young Writers we have celebrated the awesome power of creative writing, especially in young adults where it can serve as a vital method of expressing their emotions and views about the world around them. In every poem we see the effort and thought that each student published in this book has put into their work and by creating this anthology we hope to encourage them further with the ultimate goal of sparking a life-long love of writing.

Our latest competition for secondary school students, **The Power of Poetry,** challenged young writers to consider what was important to them and how to express that using the power of words. We wanted to give them a voice, the chance to express themselves freely and honestly, something which is so important for these young adults to feel confident and listened to. They could give an opinion, highlight an issue, consider a dilemma, impart advice or simply write about something they love. There were no restrictions on style or subject so you will find an anthology brimming with a variety of poetic styles and topics. We hope you find it as absorbing as we have.

We encourage young writers to express themselves and address subjects that matter to them, which sometimes means writing about sensitive or contentious topics. If you have been affected by any issues raised in this book, details on where to find help can be found at
www.youngwriters.co.uk/info/other/contact-lines

CONTENTS

Alleyn's School, Dulwich

Maxim Alexandre (12)	1
Dara Oginni (13)	2
Sophie Aggarwal (12)	4
Sienna Nicholls (12)	6
Audrey Chappell (13)	8

Clifton High School, Clifton

Sophie Mathieson (11)	9
Martha Simson (12)	10
Rebekah Pantlin (12)	13
Daisie Cade (11)	14
Charlize Hodgson (12)	16
Lyra Gilray (11)	18
Ellie Slator (11)	20
Helena Carota (12)	21
Heidi Coomes (12)	22
Emily Learmonth (11)	23
Jana Wong (12)	24

Eton Dorney Independent Therapeutic School, Dorney

Alex Bourne (15)	25
Harvey Richards (13)	26
R L (12)	28
Grace Tanner (11)	29
Kian Foster (13)	30
F J (14)	31

Golborne High School, Warrington

Lola Jackson (12)	32
Evelyn Dillingham (12)	34

Benjamin Sargent (13)	35
Seren Huish-Blakemore (12)	36
Theo Goulding (12)	37
Amora Haseldine	38
Lucas Berry (12)	39
Sophie Lawrinson (13)	40
Shaun Sanjush (12)	41
Maya Gospodaru (13)	42
Julia Lisiecka (12)	43
Tia-Louise Standen (13)	44
Oliver Crosbie-Fawcett (12)	45
Laukik Gaikwad (12)	46
Katherine Osbaldeston (12)	47

King Edward VI Community College, Totnes

Zoe Haynes (11)	48

Landau Forte College, Derby

Ella Heath (13)	50
Freya Greaney (14)	51
Leah Matthews (14)	52
Maheen Afzal (13)	53
Fizaa Amina (13)	54

Parkstone Grammar School, Poole

Lara Robinson (11)	55
Jiya Rohit (14)	56
Hattie O'Hara Day (12)	57
Keziah Jacob (11)	58
Jessica Richardson (11)	59
Francesca Lloyd (11)	60

Emily Nichols (11)	61
Leila Derwish (11)	62

Ravens Wood School, Bromley

Elliott Johnson (12)	63
Max Earwicker (11)	64

St Mary's Grammar School, Magherafelt

Odhran Neeson (13)	65
Aoife Diamond (12)	66
Cadhla Robinson (12)	68
Niamh Cunnigham (12)	69
Clodagh McBride (11)	70
Logan McCann (12)	71
Thomas McGoldrick (12)	72
Sean Birt (11)	73
Grace McCloskey (11)	74
Tiernan McLernon (12)	75
Oisin Henry (11)	76
Niamh Diamond (11)	77
Harry Armstrong (14)	78
Sophie McGarry (13)	79
Ana McClelland (14)	80
Finn Mullan (11)	81
Charlie Gribbin (11)	82
Katie Birt (11)	83
Oliver McGale (12)	84
Tyler Rogers (12)	85
Dervla Lupari (12)	86
Ella Kearney (12)	87
Caden Doris (11)	88
Dara Donnan (11)	89
Rory Smith (12)	90
Tom Harkin (13)	91
Naoise McBride (11)	92
Maggie Crozier (12)	93
Pearse Rocks (12)	94
Tom Lennon (11)	95
Leah McKinley (11)	96
Eva Merron (11)	97
Emma Loughran (12)	98
Ella Doherty (11)	99
Kielan Dodwell (13)	100
Colm McGurk (11)	101
Sonya Siriwardana (13)	102
Jonathan Teague (14) & Caolan	103
Kainagh O'Donnell (11)	104
Katherine Convery (13)	105
Tom Farmer (12)	106
Cora McPeake (12)	107
Alisha McGlone (11)	108
Eoin Michael Jeremiah Young (13)	109
Andrew Murray (11)	110
Erlandas Anisimenko (13) & Malachy	111
Oliver Nelson (11)	112
Hayden Hughes (11)	113

Tarporley High School, Tarporley

Indigo Tarplee-Williams (15)	114
Mia Anderson (11)	115
Connie Maclennan (11)	116
Summer Johnson (11)	117
Maisie Jones (11)	118

THE POEMS

Red Raven

Phantom, phoenix, flying fire,
Both silhouette and sun,
Soaring o'er the highest spire,
Greatest glider: you're the one.
You are not an eagle,
Yet nor are you a crow,
You are not so regal,
As the other birds would know.
Feasting on the fallen,
Wheeling 'cross the sky,
Always are you solemn,
For you know the day you'll die.
But will you be reborn?
Or disappear into the ages?
Will thine feathers quills adorn,
Or see you wiped from history's pages?
Whether will you ride, red raven,
Windborne to the sunset sea,
Or cower here like faithless craven?
Which one, I cannot guarantee.

Maxim Alexandre (12)
Alleyn's School, Dulwich

My Meadow

Walking along the meadows one day, I sang a dulcet tune.
The grass was wet with dew; the flowers in full bloom.
A bright array of colours, they swayed from side to side,
Smiling from ear to ear, I glowed at them with pride.
The further I got, the deeper within, it started raining hard.
The pitter-patter was constant, the droplets looked like shards.
however, it seemed to help the plants, and they surely grew.
Grinning from ear to ear, I took that as my cue.

I gathered a bunch of roses, and all that I could see,
Our sun gleamed happily, Heaven shone on me;
Spinning in the grass, twirling in the rain,
I put them in my basket, feeling not at all mundane.
My dress swirled melodiously around me,
The leaves singing a sweet summer song in the soft breeze.
All I could think of was how beautiful was this paradise,
And how I had such a happy life.

Walking along the meadows one day, I noticed something was wrong,
Everything was different, the secret I was not let on.
The once green grass was now murky and muddy, trodden on in fact,
The flowers scattered everywhere, barely even intact.

The once tranquil place was now bustling and bursting with noise,
My great big sunflower meek now, no longer held with poise.
I turned away in confusion, blinking back some tears,
Sweating and gulping continuously, as I faced my biggest fears.

Walking along the meadows one day, the place was a new scene,
With builders and tall people, who looked sinister and mean.
What are they doing here? I thought as I walked,
And one of them noticed me, which made me feel distraught.
They had dark brown hair and glowing, green eyes,
And they stomped over to me, which to m by surprise,
"What are you doing here, kid? You need to go home!"
I ran away crying, so small and alone.

Dreaming about my meadow one day, I sang my usual song,
And pondered and pondered for ages, of why this all went wrong.
I could not bear to stay away, even the thought of it caused me pain.
No more flowers for me, no more dancing in the rain?
What was I to do? Sit here and pout?
That was not an option. I needed to get out.
Sneaking out cautiously, I jogged to my usual spot,
Which was now no longer a meadow, but a business parking lot.

Dara Oginni (13)
Alleyn's School, Dulwich

Worldly Dreaming

Swinging on the emerald vines,
Through the dappled sunlight,
Zigzagging around the trees in lines,
For gorillas, this was their dream.

Colourful shoals swimming in sapphire,
Currents softly dragging them,
Past the coral, higher and higher,
For fish, this was their dream.

Paw-prints embedded in the snow,
Flakes falling from the sky,
Mountain tops with an angelic glow,
For snow leopards, this was their dream.

A safe environment in which to sleep,
Eating leafy greens all day,
No fire to make them burn and weep,
For koalas, this was their dream.

Zero gunshots ringing in their ears,
Tusks only for themselves,
A grassland Savannah with minimal fears,
For rhinos, this was their dream.

But wait - it's not too late to change it,
We can stop the madness we created,
Change everything, bit, by bit, by bit,
For humans, *this* should be our dream.

Sophie Aggarwal (12)
Alleyn's School, Dulwich

The Spider

Droplets tenderly beaded
Upon the spider's web,
Smelt of a crisp rise of day,
One to "spider" away.

A curious hand
Pulls away the finest threads,
Unknowing of the desolation.
Debris falls like volcano ashes
For the vast destruction
Of the Earth's rage to a spider's concoction.

Despised and swept away
By monstrous bristles of broom,
Huge screams send spider scurrying away
Cast into corners,
And there, in the darkness
They begin.

Weaving and swirling
Their spindly legs, needles with thread,
Spinning satin on skeletal legs,
Concocting spirals of silk.
Draped upon the ceiling,
Insects small and big are trapped
In this anatomy of fear.

Droplets tenderly beaded
Upon the spider's web,
Smelt of a crisp rise of day,
One to "spider" away.

Sienna Nicholls (12)
Alleyn's School, Dulwich

The Environment

What would happen
If it all fell apart?
Beauty, a distant dream.
Flames painting the picture of our world,
Green, an unknown colour.
Creatures howling for mercy,
Calling to the monsters that named themselves humans.
Industry spreading like a lie,
That we all try to run from.
Our future seems doomed,
We can't hide from the truth.
The truth that may well end us.

Audrey Chappell (13)
Alleyn's School, Dulwich

A Call To Action!

I don't know about you,
But I miss what we used to do,
Taking care, not throwing away,
What we could use another day.

It's probably because we think we're too cool,
To "care" about being so cruel,
Now we think it's just a joke,
So what, we threw that can of Coke?

No one's going to die because of me,
But what we need so desperately,
Is the help of the new and coming generation.
Yeah, we should be the inspiration!

All you need to do is this:
Reduce, reuse, recycle, it's hard to miss,
People, we've got to do our part,
Stop that littering and use your heart!

Sophie Mathieson (11)
Clifton High School, Clifton

The Rose And The Passion Flower

Some say I'm a thorny
flower of battle;
to some extent, I see a
truth through their lie:
I do have thorns and
reaching tentacles that curl
with disgust.
I am associated with war,
my flowers, the colour of spite,
blood.
However, a certain beauty
shines through:
I have defence,
I have attack,
I am strong and bold and rich,
full of colour and life.
Not only red but a sparkling
crimson, a pure white.
I am Rose.

My name sounds superior,
has a type of ring to it.
I create fruit that shine
orange like the dazzling sun

and my flowers are from
another world.
Purple, white, yellow
delicate and unique,
I practically sing myself, my
arms dancing in the gentle
breeze.
The aura around me glows and
swirls,
my vines creep up the wall;
snakes hissing a warning,
I smile, breathe in the cool air.
Wow, I really am a marvel.
I was born for this.
I was born a Passion Flower.

Within my beauty lies stealth;
slowly I creep like bird to prey,
I'm entwined, my body
suffocated.
Life is becoming short-lived,
I let out a strangled cry.
It uses all my strength,
I push, I pull, weakened.
The defence mechanism is in
full swing.
I should have suspected that.
Finally, a win.

My thorns:
Rescue, relief.
My feelers reach out;
determined fingers that
grab.
I pull myself up,
I'm being pushed down, I can only hold on so long.
Darkness is near,
I'm nearly there,
just a little bit further.
I curl my vines around the
stem.
There's nothing I can do.
I'm lost.
Harer, harder.
One more shot.
I jolt upwards.
Pain, like night,
I recoil
And run.
They're gone.
Away.
Sweet.
Taste.
Victory.

Martha Simson (12)
Clifton High School, Clifton

The War

Anger, passion, fear.
What do these words mean?
They are all there,
Just cannot be seen.

While children are cosy,
Asleep at night,
Soldiers relentlessly run and fight
To defend their country,
But mainly stay alive.

Their minds are ruined,
Their bodies are wrecked.
Bang!
And all are tortured,
For the majority of them,
To death.

No one could stand up,
Oh no,
One step out of line,
And they had it in for you.

Loose lips sink ships,
Keep those feelings in,
It would damage your soul,
And all of you within.

Rebekah Pantlin (12)
Clifton High School, Clifton

Hedgehog In My Garden

There's a hedgehog in my garden
and it will not go away,
I've asked several times
and she just says, "Not today!"

I tried to raise awareness,
for I only want the best,
but when I went to see her,
she grouched, "I couldn't care less!"

I'm getting really mad,
and feeling really tense,
so I grabbed a spade from the back,
and chucked her round the fence.

"Why, little hedgehog? I know you want to sleep!
But I really must confess,
you're causing a ton of stress!
And you may think I'm not being that kind,
but I won't always be there to save your behind!"

You may wonder, what's the fuss about?
Well, it's all to do with my little dachshund, Dolly,
who would tear her apart with her little snout.
It's happened before; chickens, hedgehogs and more!
She is bred to attack,

So little hedgehog, I will warn you once more,
"You really must watch your back!"

Daisie Cade (11)
Clifton High School, Clifton

Innocent Animals

The sea, the sky, the birds that fly,
the wind, the change, the range
of the arrow, piercing the sky, hitting bullseye!

They packed their bags,
off they went,
into the woods,
the time they spent...
Chasing the innocent,
it was done,
"Shot!" *Bang, bang!*
Proud they were,
to them... it was fun.

Only to them,
did they see,
poaching was, indeed, legally,
not evil, vile, what you call sport,
an amusing, mocking hunting ground,
not a last resort.

Time passed by,
on they went,
the same method,
the same concept.
They did not prevent
what was going to happen

later in the future,
they wouldn't,
they couldn't forget
their regret...

Charlize Hodgson (12)
Clifton High School, Clifton

Squirrels

Swifter than an arrow,
Lighter than a shadow,
Up the wood it hides,
Through the leaves it flies,
Towards the endless sky,
A gleaming, precious prize,
A deep mahogany shell,
A delicious, enticing smell,
It grabs the nut and runs,
Jumping for the fun.

It leaps through the dark,
With the tail of a question mark,
It scampers to the ground,
Observing the world around,
Then across the grass, it sees,
A deadly rivalry,
Another squirrel has come,
To steal the nut and run,
The rival dashes,
And the other squirrel snatches,
It takes the nut up the tree,
Hoping to be free
Of this terrible thief,
And to have relief,

Or just a moment to eat
The wonderful, tasty treat.

Lyra Gilray (11)
Clifton High School, Clifton

Willow

W illow proud on the hill,
 I n comes the cutter,
 L umber, firewood, timber,
 L ow on the ground soon.
O ut of the cherished river,
W ould you truly fell me, cutter?

 C ould I really have come to fell this tree?
U mbrella of life, symphony of song,
 T his country of creatures,
 T his tree will save me yet.
 E ach branch, each leaf, has a life.
 R each out to me willow, and set me free.

Ellie Slator (11)
Clifton High School, Clifton

Snails

Snail, oh snail, wouldn't you love to be fast,
So you wouldn't be last,
Snail, oh snail, people step on you, hurt you,
When maybe you just want to go to the loo,
Snail, oh snail, please drop things you can't eat,
Which causes you to have defeat,
Snail, oh snail, you belong in the environment,
You're part of it too, we all thrive in it,
Snail oh snail, you deserve to be loved,
I wish I could give you a great big hug.

Helena Carota (12)
Clifton High School, Clifton

Climate Conflict

We say we do better,
Cut trees down to make deserts wetter.
Anger solves nothing, yet protests work,
People screaming and going berserk!
But if a girl in a coat can make such a change
When we're still deciding to sign that page,
Who is this war against? Are they okay?
Why don't they want air and green spaces to play?
The problem is solved, who will listen?
But don't just listen, do,
The change is up to you!

Heidi Coomes (12)
Clifton High School, Clifton

Invasion

Humans invade as the animals are betrayed,
Fear is rising in their eyes, for it is humans they despise,
Up, up goes the fire, for it is fields humans wish to acquire,
A wandering tiger has forgot, that intruding humans' homes will get it shot,
Yet humans can trample all over their homes
And expect them not to roam.

Emily Learmonth (11)
Clifton High School, Clifton

Should I Save The Earth?

I always wonder
If I should save the Earth.
I often ponder,
Why I need to move forth.
Should I take action,
When the Earth is in danger?
I think I should participate,
To be one of the rangers.
Because if I don't lend a hand,
The Earth will come to an end.

Jana Wong (12)
Clifton High School, Clifton

The Future Of Us

Trees are cut down
The sea level's rising
Oil's in our ocean
No wonder the planet's dying

The ice caps are melting
The polar bears are losing their homes
It's so sad to see
But we're still on our phones

We're too blind to realise
What we are doing
The temperature is increasing
We can't see what we are losing

Disposable plastics
Bottles and straws
Turtles are choking
And we are the cause

Turn your lights off
Take a bike or the bus
Recycle your rubbish
Or there will be no future for us.

Alex Bourne (15)
Eton Dorney Independent Therapeutic School, Dorney

Judgement

They say that you're all different,
Then they say that we're the same.
You're always getting judged if you don't play their game.
Shame goes to the ones who have a choice to be different,
Called crazy when you have a voice,
Which is different than the things that their hivemind is coded to say.
The things that happen every day are all the same,
When you have an opinion, you're no fun,
They put dirt on your name,
They try and throw you away.
If you're a mindless slave
Who's on their page,
Nobody minds this, they want you to stay,
So they can use you,
Abuse you,
When you're not looking.
Then they grab you and chuck you out
When you have something else cooking.
The truth you told
Will be told in a different way.
They're all stupid,
They're programmed to do this.
These NPCs have no brains.
The youth is getting dumb and dumber
Every single day,

It's unfair,
Like a haunting dream.
When you boost your self-esteem
And build an ego,
They'll call you overconfident and cocky.
I've been down that road, so trust me,
It's really rocky.
Fighting my inner demons like I'm a sci-fi Rocky.
All this pent-up hate and anger.
It's so hard to handle.
I had to wait so long
Till someone else could come and light my candle.
I'm, slowly giving up,
Hoping someone else could hold my mantle.
I have it all,
I have someone to ask, "What's up?"
But even after Judgement Day,
I almost feel like giving up.

Harvey Richards (13)
Eton Dorney Independent Therapeutic School, Dorney

Act Now!

Why do women have to cover their hair?
Why should gay people hide their sexuality?
Why do we need plastic packaging?
Why should disabled people be picked on?
Why does the government steal our money?
Why should the Earth pay for our mistakes?

Everything has got to change now!
We must act now!
We must stop these political monsters now!

No war!
No discrimination!
No litter!
No hiding!
No bullying!
No injustice!

No pain, no gain.
Act now!

R L (12)
Eton Dorney Independent Therapeutic School, Dorney

Bad Plastic In The Ocean

I believe we can save
the animals from dying
by putting all the plastic in the bin.
I can see all the animals are crying
the plastic is being stuck in their fins!
The plastic was caught
in the turtle's shell and
it just made me want to yell.
We need to take all the plastic
out of the sea
or I'll see no turtles when I'm thirty.
Recycling our plastic
will save the planet and
the ocean will thank us
when we save it!

Grace Tanner (11)
Eton Dorney Independent Therapeutic School, Dorney

Pollution

Petrol is not the best,
You're polluting the planet,
Just give us a break.

Plastic bottles, go away,
You're not helping
In any way.

Someone make a poll,
So we can get coal
Out of this world.
You're not useful,
You're a risk,
You're scaring little kids.

Help us now,
Help us later,
But it's our duty to
Make this world even better.

Kian Foster (13)
Eton Dorney Independent Therapeutic School, Dorney

Polluting Passion

Beneath the clouds, crowds are formed,
From fury to anger,
To disbelief,
The Great Barrier Reef,
People trying
But know they're dying,
Toleration towards the technology,
Apologies being formed,
Deformed brains
Thinking of nothing,
While the icebergs are shrinking
From my point of view,
For me to get through
This lying life.

F J (14)
Eton Dorney Independent Therapeutic School, Dorney

Don't Ever Let Anyone Drag You Down

We are all wondering how others feel,
but we lose ourselves to reality,
forgetting about yourself and your emotions.
We all want to be ready for the day,
full of energy,
but sometimes the
slightest comment
can tear you down,
giving you a negative mindset.
You will always think you're not good enough,
pretty enough,
beautiful enough,
but no one feels perfect.
You may get picked on,
but the truth is,
everyone is beautiful
and unique, in their own skin,
even the bully is insecure.
Even if you're gay, straight, trans,
insecure, isolated or different,
everyone is different.
No one walks around feeling brave,
strong and fearless every day,

but remember you are you
and no one can take you
and your characteristics away.
Ignore it,
you are you,
and no one can stop that,
not even horrible haters!

Lola Jackson (12)
Golborne High School, Warrington

Plastic Pollution

P ollution is hurting sea life.
L ots of plastic is killing the coral reefs.
A single microplastic can harm multiple species in a food chain.
S ingular people can try and improve the seas.
T ime is running out!
I s this really our fate?
C an you help sea life?

P ollution is hurting sea life.
O nly we can make a change.
L et us help the ocean survive its crisis.
L itter is killing our dolphins, sharks and turtles.
U nbelievable amounts of plastic are in the sea.
T ime is running out!
I magine the hills of plastic in the seas.
O nly we can make a change.
N o, we do not have another world.

Evelyn Dillingham (12)
Golborne High School, Warrington

Bullies Of The World

To the bullies of this town,
And to the bullies of all the rest,
Stop pushing the weaker down,
It's like pushing a baby bird out of its nest,
From far up in that tree.

I have been bullied myself,
And I know others who have.
It feels like you've been pushed aside,
Like an old toy on a shelf.
Forcing those weaker to hide.
This is needing to be stopped,
Not ignored, not overlooked and not regularised.

Schools, clubs, workplaces and bullies of the world,
Stop this now, stop this here.
Keep innocent people safe from this horrible feeling.
Don't make them leave home with the fear of bleeding.
Stop the fear. Stop the violence. Stop the bullying.

Benjamin Sargent (13)
Golborne High School, Warrington

Going On Holiday For The First Time

The excitement is building.
It's almost time to leave.
I have packed all my essentials
As I lift my suitcase with a heave.

The queue to check-in is like a long, winding snake.
As we hand in our passports and load up my case,
And head for security as our trip builds up pace.

I look out of the window, I see a great plane.
We get ready to board, am I in the right lane?
As I climb aboard, I search for my seat,
I sit next to the window, I stretch my legs and feet.

We have finally arrived at the place where we will stay.
Time to unpack, hit the pool and play.
Suncream and sunglasses are on,
As I float on my lilo and soak up the sun.

Seren Huish-Blakemore (12)
Golborne High School, Warrington

Poem About My Hero, Harry Kane

Left foot, right foot, off the head
"One season wonder" comments put to bed
The more he plays, he keeps getting better
The perfect player, the ultimate goal-getter.

Golden boot two years in a row
Harry Kane with a goal-scoring show
"He's one of our own," the faithful sing
Give him the ball and goals he will bring.

What a player, what a man
If anyone can, Harry can
His class is undoubtedly now to be seen
A constant threat, to any team.

Goals, goals and goals galore
Give it to Harry
And he will score
Hat-tricks are rare
They come and go
Not for Harry
Two in a row.

Theo Goulding (12)
Golborne High School, Warrington

Climate Change

Climate change is a big problem and it's not funny,
All people care about is spending their money.
Global warming is coming,
But we will see the sun and the moon,
Now look around and see what you've done,
We're killing the world and it's not fun.
Our world is disintegrating,
We need to reintegrate,
So let's assist our world,
And tackle climate change together.

Our world is dying,
People, change your ways,
Save our world,
Before it is too late,
To help our future generations.

Amora Haseldine
Golborne High School, Warrington

The RAF In WWII

WWII is thrown around a lot
In movies
On TV
In books

But not many talk about how important the RAF were in winning the war
The Avro Manchester
The Lancaster
The Spitfire
We engineered to our heart's desire

Our brave aircrews
Who knew that what they were getting into was huge

Sortie after sortie
Fight after fight
The air forces' numbers were getting light
But they fought and fought with all their might
Knowing full well the enemies would bite.

Lucas Berry (12)
Golborne High School, Warrington

Never Go Down

When things go wrong, as they will,
Always try to keep uphill,
When things go wrong in town,
Never go down,
You will go through many bumpy roads,
But you should never go down.

You are great and amazing,
Never let anyone tell you different,
You can have anything you want
If you only believe in yourself,
You are loved all around,
And I am sure anyone would agree,
Nothing will bring you down.

Sophie Lawrinson (13)
Golborne High School, Warrington

Racism

You push me away,
You push me to the ground,
You mock me for who I am,
But I will always get back up,

I am different,
So you use that as my weakness,
But I will use it as my strength,
And I will always fight back,

You will call me names,
You will hurt me,
You will talk behind my back,
But I will stand up,
And no one and nothing can stop me.

Shaun Sanjush (12)
Golborne High School, Warrington

Beautiful Romania

What would I do
Without you?
My love for you
Is unbreakable,
As some
Say otherwise.
The stories about you,
Bad or good,
I will still
Love you.
My story about you
Is nothing but good,
I miss your smell,
I miss your safety,
I miss your food.
Oh, Romania,
My beautiful Romania.
What can I do
Without you?

Maya Gospodaru (13)
Golborne High School, Warrington

School

Sometimes school is hard to get through,
Sometimes people may disrespect you,
But have you ever been sat in class,
Wondering if you could surpass
The thought of failing in school?
Your parents in disapproval,
But most importantly,
Your dream job being unachievable.

Julia Lisiecka (12)
Golborne High School, Warrington

Nature

Nature is everywhere,
Nature is all around us.
Animals, big or small
Or plants that grow very tall.
Nature is a part of us,
Whilst the bees buzz,
Flowers bloom within the day,
As the fish swim through the bay.

Tia-Louise Standen (13)
Golborne High School, Warrington

Planes

The thought of flying a plane,
Would just be so insane,
Travelling through the sky,
Making my way up high,
Soaring through the clouds,
Wow, what a thrill,
This is so brill!

Oliver Crosbie-Fawcett (12)
Golborne High School, Warrington

Oppression

A haiku

A caged seed am I
My mother, my sweet captor
Mother, let me grow.

Laukik Gaikwad (12)
Golborne High School, Warrington

Endangered Species
A haiku

The Amur leopard
Thirty-five to forty-five
Left living in wild.

Katherine Osbaldeston (12)
Golborne High School, Warrington

Earth's Melody

Wind blowing against the trees
Earth's melody
The sound of joyful buzzing bees
Earth's melody
A stomp of an elephant parade
Earth's melody
An effervescent waterfall cascade
Earth's melody
A loud rooster in the morning
Earth's melody
A wild lion roaring
Earth's melody
An abrupt dog bark
Earth's melody
A sharp, red fire spark
Earth's melody
But what if there was no Earth song
No hum or whistle for birds to sing along
No joy in listening to nature quietly at night
Just silent stars staring back at us so bright
Not even a hushed cat meow at the door
Soon there will be no Earth's melody to live for
There is no later, it must be now
We mustn't let the Earth take its final bow

You've left it up to us to find the solution
There are too many problems, just like pollution.

Zoe Haynes (11)
King Edward VI Community College, Totnes

Breezy Thief

The slowly faded colour, fading as days go by
From green to red
Leaves dashing through the windy sky
The Breezy Thief snatching them from their branch
Prancing around our feet

Falling above our head
Awaiting for three seasons in-between to pass by
Allowing the Breezy Thief to strike again
Causing leaves to go soaring through the
Windy sky.

Ella Heath (13)
Landau Forte College, Derby

Identity

Who am I?
How can I be true to myself
When everything, everyone, is fake?

Filters, Photoshop,
Catfishes,
Make us insecure.

Haters, toxicity,
Trolls,
Make us insecure.

We hide behind a screen,
Behind a reflection
We refuse to see.

Who are we?

Freya Greaney (14)
Landau Forte College, Derby

Sleeping

S lumbered into the abyss
L ying in my bed
E xtremely tired
E valuating my thoughts
P assing on a yawn
I nvading the depth of my mind
N ever waking up
G reatest sleep of my life.

Leah Matthews (14)
Landau Forte College, Derby

Types Of Friendships

Some are real
Some are fake
Some end
Some don't
Some are hard
Some are easy
Some may flourish
Some may wither
Some bright
Some dull
Some still exist
Some I still miss.

Maheen Afzal (13)
Landau Forte College, Derby

Friendships

It's complicated
It needs loyalty
It needs trust
But sometimes you can't get that
They become two-faced
They become snakes
Untruthful
Unfaithful
Stay awake.

Fizaa Amina (13)
Landau Forte College, Derby

The Shadows

At first, it's nothing, just a natter of words
Pins meant to poke you, the occasional tease
But when the sun falls, the scales tip
You feel a cold dread, a tightness in your stomach

Fear washes over you, pushes you in to drown in your screams
Words pierce your skin as the walls close in
There's no one there
No one there to hear you - you are alone, forced to face the shadows...

...Until you let the light in
The river of emotions pour out
The tightness eases...
...as a loved one holds you up

The night has ended, the spring has come
Confidence blooms, yellow, pink and green
Sunlight washes in, shadows fading
As you finally let the words go
The shadow is no more.

Lara Robinson (11)
Parkstone Grammar School, Poole

What Have We Done?

Floods and fires,
Disaster after disaster, and yet nothing has changed.
Every day we dig this "hole" deeper and deeper, inching closer to the end;
What is this "hole" you may ask?
It's the end which humans have shaped for ourselves.
Human extinction.

Our once blue, thriving planet, is now crying for help,
And yet we ignore it.
We only indulge in our wants and desires.
We are fuelled by the villain of all of this,
Greed.
The want for more and more, but only for our current benefit.

What have we done?
What are we going to do?

Jiya Rohit (14)
Parkstone Grammar School, Poole

Just Being Me

Just being me,
It's the hardest person to be.
With long, brown locks.
And an obsession with odd socks.
Nobody really likes me,
They make fun of my height, see.
My need to talk,
The pace of my walk.
They say I can't sing,
And laugh at me for trying.
How I'm smart,
The lack of skills I have in art.
But all the things they say,
Can't ruin my day,
My optimism is gleaming,
The fire in my heart is steaming.
I will rise up against the bad,
No matter what, I will try to be glad,
Because just being me, is the best person to be!

Hattie O'Hara Day (12)
Parkstone Grammar School, Poole

The Problem Of Bullying...

You wake up, the sky is dark and gloomy
You don't know what will happen
You are dreading going to school
You don't know why this is happening
You wish it could end
It's all very confusing and you need some help
But there's no one at home
You feel like the world is ending
You see the children outside laughing and playing
You're jealous inside
When you walk to school, your every step takes as much strength as possible

And then you meet them
The big gang of older children
The one that makes you feel miserable every day...

Keziah Jacob (11)
Parkstone Grammar School, Poole

The Wish Of A Turtle

I glide through the water, clear and blue,
Then suddenly, I see something new,
Brightly coloured plastics, covering the ground,
Remind me of something I once found,
It was drifting through the water, I first thought it was a fish,
I wave to say, "Hello!" but it turns out it was rubbish,
I look again at the colourful plastic, wanting it to disappear,
For I have one enormous fear,
That the litter will stay there forever and ever,
Remove it, we can never,
The only ones who can,
Are the humans,
They can.

Jessica Richardson (11)
Parkstone Grammar School, Poole

Nothing I Can Do

The sun falls from the sky,
And the moon rises,
Bringing with it another night of terrors,
Bombs rain down,
And fires climb even higher,
People crying,
Always crying,
And I am helpless to stop it,
There's nothing I can do,
As I watch my brothers march off to war,
Ready to face a bullet for our country,
And all I can do is cry,
There's nothing I can do.

Francesca Lloyd (11)
Parkstone Grammar School, Poole

Help

Our seas, littered,
Our animals, dying,
Our world is falling apart.
Humans have destroyed everything,
Have we got no hearts?

Somebody has to do something,
Stand up, make a difference,
Because global warming will not stop,
Until we start to listen.

So help our dying planet,
Our animals, our seas.
Do it for future generations.
Please.

Emily Nichols (11)
Parkstone Grammar School, Poole

Something Precious

When you lose something precious, you feel lost,
When you lose something precious, you feel sad,
When you lose something precious, you feel like your world is gone,
But when you find something precious, it can change your world forever.

Leila Derwish (11)
Parkstone Grammar School, Poole

Memory Lane

Taking a trip down memory lane,
A once calmer reality,
I see the fishes swim without their upcoming catastrophe,
I see the wildlife jump from tree to tree,
But not fleeing from fire, instead, they are free.
I see the plants grow from little seeds,
Not knowing about their future needs,
But when the time had come,
There became an awful limit of fun.

However, now with the veil of pollution,
There begins a new revolution,
With the filthy ocean,
There creates a wild commotion,
With the disappointing deforestation,
It causes a poor salvation.

Falling back to my circumstances,
I breathe in and out,
In and out,
My flippers begin to tremble,
I look up at the dreamy atmosphere,
As it becomes further away from me,
The freezing white floor beneath me splits apart,
Dragging me down into the waves.

Elliott Johnson (12)
Ravens Wood School, Bromley

Unfinished Stories

As the plastic lurks, closer and closer,
The fish doesn't realise the danger,
And despite the innocence of the fish,
It's gliding closer and closer,
To the end of its unfinished story.

The fish rapidly swinging their fins around,
Gasping for fresh water to breathe in,
As chances of survival seem to be gliding
Further and further away into the water.

But so soon,
The fish's tail closes to an end,
When something thought "harmless",
Has brought an end to an innocent soul.

Max Earwicker (11)
Ravens Wood School, Bromley

Climate Change And Environment

C ars are producing too many fumes.
L ater on, we will be too warm.
I f we don't do something, our planet will suffer.
M aybe we could recycle to tidy it up,
A nd then we can save animals and money.
T urtles can freely swim with no plastic danger.
E veryone can make a difference, so why don't you?

C an't we all just become more eco-friendly?
H eat trapped inside is going to destroy us.
A ny consideration for what you do makes a difference.
N ever should we disrespect our planet and destroy it.
G et out there and help your local place.
E veryone should spread awareness.

Odhran Neeson (13)
St Mary's Grammar School, Magherafelt

This Is Our World

This is our world,
This is unacceptable,
This is hurting us,
Pollution is not a joke!

This beautiful planet,
Being destroyed by mankind,
Everywhere you look there are more
And more fossil fuels being burnt.

This is our world,
This is unacceptable,
This is hurting us,
Climate change is not a joke!

This beautiful planet,
Being quite diverse,
Excluding men and women,
Black, white and disabled.

This is our world,
This is unacceptable,
This is hurting us,
Diversity is not a joke!

This is our world,
This is our responsibility,
This is not a joke,
Together we can improve it.

Aoife Diamond (12)
St Mary's Grammar School, Magherafelt

Deforestation

When you're sleeping at night, what do you hear?
Is it the rain falling down or the birds cheeping near?
You may be thinking of the trees blowing in the breeze,
sprinkling the ground with their leaves.
But wait, where have they gone?
The only trees I see are the ones on my lawn!

Trees, trees, everywhere.
So beautiful that I start to stare!
Saws, saws, everywhere.
Coming from their evil lair.
Why are they cutting the trees down,
causing everyone to wear a frown?

All of us need trees to breathe,
so why are they cutting them down and making them leave?
We need trees to combat pollution,
so cutting them down is not a solution!

Cadhla Robinson (12)
St Mary's Grammar School, Magherafelt

Our World

Our world is changing, the bushes are burning,
The temperature is rising,
And the weather is turning,
Some people still don't believe that it's true,
Have you seen the pit that we've dug ourselves into?
What do we do?
I really don't know,
But whatever it is, we're being too slow!
So let's speed up the process before it's too late,
To get a new world, we must open a gate.
"And if there isn't a gate?" you ask, and I'll say,
"We build our own, so we see another day."
We all have to take part to save the planet,
So let's do it now.
Before it crumbles to granite.

Niamh Cunnigham (12)
St Mary's Grammar School, Magherafelt

Problems With The Planet

Let's start off with deforestation
And how people chop down trees.
Trees give birds and animals a home,
Trees give us air to breathe.
I understand that you need wood
To build tables and furnish homes,
But just remember that forests are an animal's place to roam.

Next, I'm going to talk a bit about pollution,
But when there's a problem,
There's always a solution.
We need to reduce our carbon footprint,
We need to take action and must ensure it.

This is the end of my poem
And the message is clear to see.
We need to stop pollution
And reduce the chopping down of trees.

Clodagh McBride (11)
St Mary's Grammar School, Magherafelt

The Future Is In Our Hands

E veryone needs a better future
N ever waste valuable resources
V arious amounts of COs are being released into our atmosphere
I n the UK, over 550 million tonnes of CO_2 is released every year
R eady is what we should be, for cleaner energy
O nly use valuable energy when it's a must
N ever throw litter anywhere except in the bin
M oving forward, let's aim for a cleaner environment
E arth needs this change, if we stand together, the future is brighter!
N ature is beautiful, let's keep it that way
T ime is running out, and of that, we have no doubt.

Logan McCann (12)
St Mary's Grammar School, Magherafelt

Horrible Pollution

Horrible pollution, what can we do?
Our beloved ocean, getting covered with rubbish,
this is a disaster and we must do something soon.

The poor sea creatures think it's food,
just to realise it's nothing good,
they choke on the plastic and start to suffer,
all because of a simple plastic bag.

But we can put an end to it,
by putting your rubbish in the bin,
it's good for the ocean, it's not a sin.

I hope you learned something from this,
just don't litter, don't insist.
Horrible pollution, what can we do?
Put your rubbish in the bin, that is what we'll do.

Thomas McGoldrick (12)
St Mary's Grammar School, Magherafelt

The Environment

T he world is dying
H elp us look after the world
E ndangered animals at stake

E ven though they're animals, they should still be saved
N ever litter
V ery important task
I n the troubles of the world
R unning the world is hard but they could do a better job
O ut of all the world, there's not much trying
N ever use fossil fuels if possible
M ake use of materials
E ven if there's no bin, keep hold of rubbish
N ever burn plastic
T o make sure the world stays safe.

Sean Birt (11)
St Mary's Grammar School, Magherafelt

Our Planet Earth

What we are doing to the Earth is terrible
Climate change, global warming, everything is heating up
Too much pollution in our seas
Too many polar ice caps melting too fast

Too many animals becoming endangered
Too many trees being cut down
Snow is melting
Snow is melting so we must start protecting

We are using too much electricity
We are using too many fossil fuels
The Earth is heating up
The Earth is heating up far too fast

We need your help
We need it now
To save our Earth
To save our future.

Grace McCloskey (11)
St Mary's Grammar School, Magherafelt

'Our' Green, Luscious Land

The grass so green,
the nature so loud,
Why would you want to harm it?
Why would you punish it?
Why not try to make it better?
Help it a little bit,
if we all work harder,
we hope we can stop this mess.

The animals that live in trees
deserve to live too, and not be homeless.
The birds, beetles and you,
we all get affected by this mess,
so why, so why do you do it
take control,
corrupt and patrol
through our luscious, green land,
every little helps, but bigger helps more.
Speak up and be heard.

Tiernan McLernon (12)
St Mary's Grammar School, Magherafelt

Earth, Our Home

E arth is our planet, the place that we call home.
A place as special as Earth should be protected with all we have.
R eviving our Earth is something we should do, by using less fuel and maybe we could use less electricity too.
T o save our planet Earth, the place that we call home, we should try a lot harder or even just a bit to save the Earth and all that live within it.
H ip hip, hooray! We finally saved the Earth. Now it will live a little longer. Let's keep it up and keep our home here for generations to come.

Oisin Henry (11)
St Mary's Grammar School, Magherafelt

Our Weeping World

The Earth is dying,
The forests are crying.
What is happening to the air?
"Human beings don't care!"

As temperature increases,
Some wildlife ceases.
Fossil fuels are burning,
But are people learning?

Plastic killing sealife,
An underwater, silent strife.
An evergrowing, endangered list,
With loads of opportunities missed.

2040 - I don't think we'll make it!
Human destruction, our Earth cannot take it.
So together we must strive,
To keep our world alive.

Niamh Diamond (11)
St Mary's Grammar School, Magherafelt

Problem At Hand

The threat of climate change is always there
But it seems like no one wants to care

Something needs to happen, we need to change
To ignore this threat at hand would be deranged

The CO_2 levels are dangerously high
This isn't something that will just fly by

The ice caps are melting away
Turning to water, day by day

The ozone layer is getting thinner
The CO_2 is eating it up like dinner

If we work together we can fix the damage
That has been caused by corporate savage.

Harry Armstrong (14)
St Mary's Grammar School, Magherafelt

Fix It

The sky clear,
The water clean,
The fields are filled
With lots of green.

All is great
Till gases kill,
Acid rain falls
And oil spills.

What is being done
To help this world get better?
It used to be so much fun.

I wish that this Earth
Was as healthy as the day of its birth,
With a second chance,
We could all sing and dance.

Fix it while we can,
Before it's too late,
Our planet is being destroyed
At a very rapid rate.

Sophie McGarry (13)
St Mary's Grammar School, Magherafelt

Our Planet

Thick, black smoke drifting through our planet,
Choking and killing the humans who inhabit it.
Acid in the rain,
Air full of gas.
Oil in the ocean,
Cities full of trash.
The planet holds people accountable
For all the mess they've made,
Our planet is dying for a reason,
Pollution, litter, climate change.
Help put an end
To our planet's suffering,
Just look at its current state.
Don't let the planet
Die in your hands,
Save it before it's too late.

Ana McClelland (14)
St Mary's Grammar School, Magherafelt

Our Environment

E ndangered animals at stake
N ever use fossil fuels if possible
V ery important stuff is happening with the environment
I like pandas so we should save them
R eally take in that this is important
O ur Earth needs to be cared for
N ot enough money is donated to help the environment
M ake a change now!
E ven if they're animals, we should
N ever smoke, it hurts the environment
T he environment is important.

Finn Mullan (11)
St Mary's Grammar School, Magherafelt

Our Planet

E verything is supposed to be green, but it's all gone dark
A ir is clear, fresh and healthy, now it's dark, thick and unclean
R uthless people littering, destroying the planet with their rubbish
T he people waiting for an environmental clock to stop, but everyone is kept in suspense
H ell is breaking loose, fires, littering and melting ice caps, but we can help. Just walk, don't drive, put litter in bins. This will all help. A little change can mean a lot.

Charlie Gribbin (11)
St Mary's Grammar School, Magherafelt

Our Planet

I am the Earth,
I am your little planet,
Please take care of me,
Reduce your use of plastic,
Throw your rubbish in the bin,
Not on my lovely land,
I am your little house,
So treat me with respect,
Keep me spick-and-span and
Spotless, use less water,
If we don't act now,
We will have no planet,
I will be gone,
Honestly, it's not that hard,
Simply recycle,
And you can help too!
We can fight global warming,
Help save our Earth.

Katie Birt (11)
St Mary's Grammar School, Magherafelt

A Solution To Pollution

When you see litter on the street
In places where you'd like to meet
There's something each of us can do
To keep our world green and blue.

The Earth needs us to change our ways
So we can enjoy better days
When our actions make pollution
Remember, there is an alternative solution.

It's time to think about our environment
So we can enjoy our retirement.

Let's take time to make amends
So we can see pollution end.

Oliver McGale (12)
St Mary's Grammar School, Magherafelt

The Turtles

F eel for the animals and plant life
U nderstand what you are doing to the environment
L ive cautiously, don't litter
L ove your environment and keep it safe

O f all things, don't destroy life
F ind life in small things

L ater on, it will be too late to change
I n life, find beauty
F ollow inspiring people's footsteps to help the world
E njoy life to the fullest.

Tyler Rogers (12)
St Mary's Grammar School, Magherafelt

Stop The Waste

Have you ever looked at trees
And seen their amazing beauty?
If you have, you know that their protection,
It's a stern and sacred duty.
When you see litter in the streets
And the air smells of pollution,
When you feel like it's all piling up,
Remember there is a solution.
We have to stop
That is all
Or else our world is what will fall.
We all need to reduce our waste,
Let's do it now with plenty of haste.

Dervla Lupari (12)
St Mary's Grammar School, Magherafelt

What I Think About Climate Change

C is for... Climate change is a very serious matter
L is for... Love the planet Earth, don't harm it
I is for... If people keep littering, the environment will die
M is for... Miles of melting ice sheets.
A is for... Actions can lead to serious consequences for the climate.
T is for... Temperatures are rising globally
E is for... Everyone can do their part to stop climate change.

Ella Kearney (12)
St Mary's Grammar School, Magherafelt

Climate Change

Our beautiful Earth is in ruin
How can we make people realise what we're doing

The situation is getting drastic
We are using too much plastic

There is far too much pollution
We need to start thinking of a solution

If every person started to be more green
More of this beautiful world could be seen

So let's put our heads together so
Future generations can enjoy this world forever.

Caden Doris (11)
St Mary's Grammar School, Magherafelt

The Earth Needs You

The Earth needs you
To change your ways,
Month by month,
Day by day.

The changes are easy.
Just look and you'll see,
The differences that can be made
By you and by me.

Single-use plastic
Lasts almost forever,
It might be cheap,
But it's not very clever.

It can end in oceans, rivers and seas.
The wind sometimes carries it
And it tangles in trees.

Dara Donnan (11)
St Mary's Grammar School, Magherafelt

The Polar Meltdown

Polar bear, polar bear
How can you survive out there
Amongst all the melting snow
You could end up trapped below

Little penguin, little penguin
How can you play out there
You love to slide along the ice
It's melting now and that's not nice

Is there anything I can do
To make life better for you
I could turn my gadgets off at night
That could help to make things right.

Rory Smith (12)
St Mary's Grammar School, Magherafelt

Gas! Gas! And An Ecstasy Of Fumbling

The world is dying,
Can't you see?
It's so very obvious,
I just want it to be freed!

As rubbish lies everywhere,
Carbon dioxide pollutes the air.
Humans lay waste by their hand,
As this gradually becomes a no-man's-land.

It all leads to destruction and despair,
As we cannot breathe this filthy air.
Every last particle will pass away,
As our lungs rot and decay.

Tom Harkin (13)
St Mary's Grammar School, Magherafelt

Environment End

From lovely flowers and tall trees,
To awful factories,
Oh just look at what the world has turned into,
From floods and droughts,
To forest fires too,
If I could stop it, what could I do?
If you could do anything, what would you do?
Round every corner and every turn,
There could be a car crash or a house about to burn.
If you could stop it,
Please stop it,
Because it could happen to you!

Naoise McBride (11)
St Mary's Grammar School, Magherafelt

Global Warming

G reat world destroyed
L and animals dying
O ur rainforests dying
B roken ice everywhere
A ntarctica melting
L ots of fire

W armer temperatures
A ll around the world, disaster strikes
R acing against time
M elting ice
I gloos gone
N orth Pole disappearing
G lobal challenges we face.

Maggie Crozier (12)
St Mary's Grammar School, Magherafelt

Around The World

Around the world, we are fighting for survival,
Around the world, people don't care,
We need to act to make it far.

Around the world, even animals know something is wrong,
Around the world, fires are burning,
The world keeps turning, we need to act fast.

Around the world, cities smell of pollution,
Around the world, cars are revving,
Buy electric cars instead.

Pearse Rocks (12)
St Mary's Grammar School, Magherafelt

Global Warming

Protecting the Earth is
a crucial challenge. You
and I have to make it
happen with water levels
rising, affecting our habitats.
We face losing family,
friends and homes,
because of flood and fire.

Fossil fuels are ruining
our lives, renewable energy
is much desired.

Planting trees is a
good idea, please
please, please protect
it now.

Tom Lennon (11)
St Mary's Grammar School, Magherafelt

Pollution, Pollution

P ollution is something we need to discuss
O h, pollution needs to stop
L ives of innocent creatures have been lost
L ives of sea creatures can be saved
U nderwater there is lots of litter
T he litter should be put into bins
I nto the bin, not the sea
O h, pollution needs to stop
N ow is the time to do something about it.

Leah McKinley (11)
St Mary's Grammar School, Magherafelt

There's No Planet B!

The air is filling with deadly gas
And we don't know how to stop it.
Well, here are some tips
For an easy fix.

Walk if you can,
It really helps,
Or even take public transport.

Recycle, don't litter,
Make our cities glitter.

So if you want to help,
Play your part, and together,
We can save our planet.
There's no Planet B!

Eva Merron (11)
St Mary's Grammar School, Magherafelt

Climate Change

C aring for the environment
L oving the Earth
I ce is melting
M aking the Earth warm
A rctic warming
T emperatures changing
E ating the ozone layer

C leaning the wildlife
H elp the Earth
A trocious heat
N ature decaying
G reenhous gases
E veryone has a place to fix it.

Emma Loughran (12)
St Mary's Grammar School, Magherafelt

The Beauty Outdoors

I weave among the leaf-filled trees,
The flowers dancing in the breeze.
I watch as a butterfly flutters by,
Everything at peace, nothing awry.
I hear the little birds sing,
They fly so high with those wings!
I smell the bluebells, what a delight!
It's all so beautiful, within my sight.
I think to myself, how lucky we are,
To see so much beauty from afar.

Ella Doherty (11)
St Mary's Grammar School, Magherafelt

Global Warming

G lobal warming
L ots of fire
O ver pollution
B iofuels running out
A ntarctica melting
L osing animals

W ater levels rising
A ustralia getting hotter
R ivers overflowing
M elting in Greenland
I ce caps melting
N orth Pole disappearing
G laciers going.

Kielan Dodwell (13)
St Mary's Grammar School, Magherafelt

Save The Future

Climate change is happening
We need to act fast
The planet's heating
The icebergs are melting
All because of us humans
We're ruining this planet
Fossil fuels are burning
Spreading pollution in the air
This needs to stop
Now
The planet is being killed by humans
Save the planet
Play your part.

Colm McGurk (11)
St Mary's Grammar School, Magherafelt

Environment

E veryone
N eeds to help the environment.
V icious gases make it hard to breathe.
I ce caps are melting.
R ays are hurting us.
O ur ozone is disappearing. It's
N ot too late to
M ake things right.
E veryone
N eeds
T o help the environment.

Sonya Siriwardana (13)
St Mary's Grammar School, Magherafelt

Autumn

The leaves falling off the trees
Autumn
The greens turning orange
Autumn
The sun going to sleep early
Autumn
The moon rising early
Autumn
The leaves falling off trees
Autumn
The coats coming out of retirement
Autumn
The hats returning off the shelves
Autumn.

Jonathan Teague (14) & Caolan
St Mary's Grammar School, Magherafelt

Our World

Our world
Do you care for our world?
Is it important to you?

Our world
Once a beautiful place
Now it's destroyed and dead

Our world
Don't you ever realise how beautiful Earth is?
One plastic bottle littered can have a big impact on the Earth.

Kainagh O'Donnell (11)
St Mary's Grammar School, Magherafelt

A Little Something

The boy asked the lady
"Why should I bother trying?
Me doing something isn't going to change the world."
The lady smiles down.
"Well, if everyone thinks like that,
There won't be any change.
A little something
Can make a little change."

Katherine Convery (13)
St Mary's Grammar School, Magherafelt

Climate

C lean up our beaches.
L itter is bad, put it in a bin.
I am doing a litter-pick at school.
M ake a difference if you can.
A rctic is melting.
T rees should be planted.
E nergy should be kept as much as possible.

Tom Farmer (12)
St Mary's Grammar School, Magherafelt

Climate Change

C hallenging the life on our planet.
L and flooding and drying out.
I f we don't act now, Earth will die!
M elting of icebergs.
A rctic heating up.
T emperatures changing.
E ndangering several species.

Cora McPeake (12)
St Mary's Grammar School, Magherafelt

The Environment

We make speeches about littering,
But nobody is listening.
We talk about global warming,
But no one thinks it's alarming.
Please just try, because it's a joke,
If you don't even realise, then you're a part of the joke.

Alisha McGlone (11)
St Mary's Grammar School, Magherafelt

There Is No Planet B

There is no Planet B,
As we all can see,
The ice is melting,
The rain is pelting,
Our Earth is heating up,
Like boiling hot water in a cup,
There is no Planet B!

Eoin Michael Jeremiah Young (13)
St Mary's Grammar School, Magherafelt

Help The Environment

H elp the world, we are struggling,
E nvironment is important, stop littering,
L isten to the news,
P lease don't litter, save our world.

Andrew Murray (11)
St Mary's Grammar School, Magherafelt

Global Warming Poem

C arbon emissions
O ver polluting the air
2 little actions.

Native polar bears
Turning extinct currently
Recycle right now.

Erlandas Anisimenko (13) & Malachy
St Mary's Grammar School, Magherafelt

Our World

A haiku

The world is our source
Without it, we would not live
Stop destroying it.

Oliver Nelson (11)
St Mary's Grammar School, Magherafelt

Climate Change
A haiku

Hot temperatures
Are changing weather patterns
All across the Earth.

Hayden Hughes (11)
St Mary's Grammar School, Magherafelt

Later Is Too Late

The air is thickening
and becoming unsterile.
The ice caps are melting
and sea levels are rising.
Polar bears have nowhere,
nowhere to live,
nowhere to roam.

Green is turning to brown,
fires burning up bush.
Trees are falling down.
Soon in the forest, there'll be nothing but hush.

We had a chance to act then,
we have a chance to act now,
but later is too late.

You've ruined the world for the next generation
with your "It doesn't matter now" and "we'll start on this date."
Now you've left it all till later
and we will soon pay.
I am afraid to say,
you've left it till later.

But later is too late.

Indigo Tarplee-Williams (15)
Tarporley High School, Tarporley

What Will Be Left?

Light, flustering, flickering leaves
bustling about in the autumn breeze.
Saving the land, saving the trees, saving the ocean, saving the bees.
Working together, standing up strong,
when will you realise, the world, we have wronged?
Warm, summer mornings, crisp, winter nights,
when will you realise the Earth has rights?
Activist groups, over water, wars and troops,
it's not really helping, please try to regroup.

No one is helping, the icebergs are melting,
"Please help me, I feel so empty,"
said the world, back in 1750.

Like a clock on a bomb, it's been so long.
What's gonna be left for us?

Mia Anderson (11)
Tarporley High School, Tarporley

Our Planet!

We need to save the planet
But what can we do?
We need to work together
And that's including you.

Our rainforests are disappearing,
Our icebergs are melting fast,
If we keep letting this happen,
These things will be in the past.

Some animals are becoming extinct,
Decreasing day by day,
The only way to stop this
Is changing our human way.

Global warming's happening,
Deforestation too,
If we don't do something about it,
There will be no Planet Earth for me or you.

Connie Maclennan (11)
Tarporley High School, Tarporley

Our Wonderful World

Mix in trees,
That sway in the gentle breeze,
Pour in flowers,
That grow in the light showers,
Whisk in plants,
And the little ants,
Add in wildlife,
That you will remember for the rest of your life.

Spoon in weather,
And the touch of a soft feather,
Stir in sun,
And have some fun,
Take away the litter,
And add some glitter,
Blend in the tweeting birds,
And the groups of animals we call 'herds'.

Summer Johnson (11)
Tarporley High School, Tarporley

Our Home

Dying slowly,
Time creeping past us,
The love for the world cannot last us.

Rainy days,
And hot ones too,
You buy a lot and waste,
Recycle your rubbish so time doesn't go faster.

Enjoy your time,
You might not have long,
Save our planet,
It's our home.

As we grow older,
The fight prolongs,
Save our home,
It's all we have got.

Maisie Jones (11)
Tarporley High School, Tarporley

Young Writers Information

We hope you have enjoyed reading this book – and that you will continue to in the coming years.

If you're the parent or family member of an enthusiastic poet or story writer, do visit our website **www.youngwriters.co.uk/subscribe** and sign up to receive news, competitions, writing challenges and tips, activities and much, much more! There's lots to keep budding writers motivated!

If you would like to order further copies of this book, or any of our other titles, then please give us a call or order via your online account.

Young Writers
Remus House
Coltsfoot Drive
Peterborough
PE2 9BF
(01733) 890066
info@youngwriters.co.uk

Join in the conversation!
Tips, news, giveaways and much more!

YoungWritersUK YoungWritersCW youngwriterscw